Still Her Spirit Sings

ISBN-13: 978-0-9760220-1-5   ISBN-10: 0-9760220-1-X
Library of Congress Cataloging Number: 2005906946

Kidzpoetz Publishing publishes books for schools.
Learn more at www.kidzpoetz.com

A percentage of the profits from the sale of this book will go to help animal causes.

www.kidzpoetz.com

Requests for permission to make copies of any part of the work should be mailed to the following address:
Kidzpoetz Publishing
P.O. Box 621
New City, New York 10956

Still Her Spirit Sings incorporates the font "Mrs. Eaves," which was designed by Zuzana Licko of Emigre c/o Bitstream Inc., MyFonts.com

Dedicated to the memory of Spirit

July 10th, 1999
Lake George, New York

For Lisa, Cassidy & Rachel

I find it just amazing
When daily I stop and think,
That she's no longer with us,
Yet still her spirit sings.

From "Her Life Runs Through Me," a poem from the book, *Lilies on the Moon*

She was the princess of the litter
Crawling on top of the other pups
That's the reason I picked her out
A pudgy pup that wobbled so proud.

Mommy wasn't pleased when we came home
That's because I didn't ask her first
She wanted me to take her back
It's funny how long that didn't last!

It wasn't too hard to choose a name
As we watched her bounce around the rooms
She soon had found the steps to climb
Spirit was the name that came to mind.

We used to bathe her in the sink
So small was she within our hands
Water soon became a good friend
The bath she jumped in time and again.

She used to sleep soundly in her crate
Then she moved into the laundry room
We tried to train her in a class
But she sure would have none of that!

As a puppy she loved to chew
Her teeth were like little sharp saws
Wood and plastic were her favorites
She never really liked the carpets.

We tried and tried to stop the chewing
But we could not get her to quit it
At last we were forced to face the fact
That for chewing Spirit had a knack.

Then one day we went for a walk
She nearly pulled us off our feet
And as we looked down at those paws
We knew our puppy was now a dog.

The garbage became very tempting
So much so we had to lock it
She would eat right off the table
Tissues, food . . . she was no angel.

Someone once said she had kind eyes
We sure didn't disagree with that
They also showed when she was sad
They also showed when she was bad.

Front door greetings were a given
When we came home from work and school
She'd have a shoe for us in her mouth
After a long day on the couch.

We'd bring her swimming in a lake
Throw a thick stick that she'd bring back
When it snowed she'd wiggle her nose
Deep in the drifts until it froze.

our dog Spirit

Time to leave the dog park

When our neighbor, Marge, lost her hair. Spirit wore her pink bandana on her head!

Spirit waits for Mommy to get home from work.

VINTON CO.
4783
555-309-6142
Spirit's 1st license tag

Pretty girl!

Sleepy Spirit

She had a wardrobe of bandanas
That she wore humbly around
her neck
From her collar hung her
tinkling tags
That made music when
her tail wagged.

Sometimes she would chase our clever cats
Around the house until they hid
But we knew she was only playing
And our cats didn't need our saving.

When it was time to say goodnight
She would plop herself on our bed
Often she would then sneak under
And snore beneath our cozy covers.

There were times when we would wake up
And hear her having a bad dream
We would force her from her slumber
What scared her we only wondered.

Then one day she ate something bad
She got sick and could barely walk
We did our best to make her better
Then buried our precious treasure.

After she died we cried and cried
For we couldn't play with her anymore
But it was more than play that we missed
More than her smile and sloppy kiss.

She didn't know how to hold a grudge
Unlike some people that we know
People can have so many flaws
The same cannot be said of dogs.

She did know how to cheer us up
On the days when we were way down
She was both friend and family
Was, is and forever shall be.

She was a center of deep love
She was a center of happiness
She taught us so much and helped us change
Spirit's sparks igniting leaping flames.

Now like fires we grow and spread
To enlighten and warm the world
With glowing tales of our mutts
Their blazing old souls guiding us.

Souls? Dogs? Is this really possible?
Since souls aren't bound by earthly years
Will we be together again
If we, too, have souls that know no end?

When a sense gives us pause to recall
We drift off into our open minds
To another time's forgotten space
Whereupon we're licked on the face.

While wet dog aroma fills the air
And paws pitter patter on the floor
Oh yes, believe with all of your heart
That our dogs are still on their guard!

They inspire our honest acts
Brightly move us to compassion
Their loyalty lives on after death
As lessons learned in our every breath

Though this tale has now been told
Words, like souls, know no end
May they comfort you through your days
Long, long after you turn this page.

Find your "Spirit."

Adopt a loving dog from a reputable animal shelter near you.
It could be one of the best decisions you've ever made.